D0437615

Cosmopolitan in Denmark

– and Other Poems about the Danes

Books by Benny Andersen:

DEN MUSIKALSKE ÅL
Poems 1960

KAMERA MED KØKKENADGANG
Poems 1962

NIKKE NIKKE NAMBO
og andre danske børnerim og remser
Children's book 1963

LILLE PETER DILLE
og andre udenlandske børnerim og remser
Children's book 1964

DEN INDRE BOWLERHAT
Poems 1964

PUDERNE
Short stories 1965

PORTRÆTGALLERI
Poems 1966

OS
Lise Roos (silhouettes) og
Benny Andersen (text) 1966

SNØVSEN OG EIGIL OG KATTEN I SÆKKEN
Children's book 1967

TYKKE-OLSEN M.FL.
Short stories 1968

DET SIDSTE ØH
Poems 1969

DEN HÆSE DRAGE
Children's comedy 1969

SNØVSEN PÅ SOMMERFERIE
Children's book 1970

LEJEMORDEREN OG ANDRE SPIL
Television and radio play 1970

HER I RESERVATET
Poems 1971

MAN BURDE BURDE
Selected poems 1971

Henning Carlsen og Benny Andersen:
MAN SKU' VÆRE NOGET VED MUSIKKEN
Film manuscript 1972

SNØVSEN OG SNØVSINE
Children's book 1972

SVANTES VISER
A story with songs 1972

BARNET DER BLEV ÆLDRE OG ÆLDRE
Essays and reminiscences 1973

UNDSKYLD HR., HVOR LIGGER
NATUREN?
Children's radio novel 1973

PERSONLIGE PAPIRER
Poems 1974

Henning Carlsen og Benny Andersen:
EN LYKKELIG SKILSMISSE
Film manuscript 1975

NOMADER MED NODER
Poems etc. 1976

UNDER BEGGE ØJNE
Poems 1978

ORFEUS I UNDERGRUNDEN
Play 1979

HIMMELSPRÆT
ELLER KUNSTEN AT KOMME
TIL VERDEN
Poems 1979

PÅ BROEN
Novel 1981

OVEN VISSE VANDE
Songs 1981

OVER SKULDEREN
Short stories 1983

SNØVSEN HOPPER HJEMMEFRA
Children's book 1984

HYMNER OG UKRUDT
Songs 1985

TIDEN OG STORKEN
Poems 1985

HYDDELIHAT
Children's comedy 1986

ANDRE SIDER
Poems 1987

Poul Dissing og Benny Andersen:
OVER ADSKILLIGE GRÆNSER
Songs 1988

LILLE PIGE MED STOR EFFEKT
Children's book 1989

CHAGALL & SKORPIONDANS
Poems, prose poems, prose etc. 1991

SNØVSEN
Children's book 1992

DENNE KOMMEN OG GÅEN
Poems, prose poems, prose 1993

SNØVSEN TA'R SPRINGET
Children's book 1994

BENNY ANDERSEN

Cosmopolitan in Denmark

– and Other Poems about the Danes

TRANSLATED BY CYNTHIA LA TOUCHE ANDERSEN
ILLUSTRATED BY MARIA BRAMSEN

BORGEN

Cosmopolitan in Denmark
– and Other Poems about the Danes
Translated by Cynthia La Touche Andersen
Originalens titel/Original Danish title:
Verdensborger i Danmark
– og andre digte om danskere
© Benny Andersen 1995
English translation © Cynthia La Touche Andersen 1995
Illustrations © Maria Bramsen 1995
Published by Borgens Forlag, Valbygaardsvej 33,
DK-2500 Copenhagen Valby
Printed by Reproset
ISBN 87-21-00357-2

1. udgave, 4. oplag 1997
First edition, fourth impression 1997

Translator's note: The translations of the poems »Smile«, »This Is«,
»Dear Friends« and »Time« are based on Alexander Taylor's versions in
Selected Poems (Princeton University Press).

CONTENTS

With special thanks to Grace & Tony Hiscocks

INTRODUCTION

At regular intervals over the years, foreign friends have asked me to give them my conception of the Danes, of Danish identity and mentality. Similarly, Danish friends have requested my views on the prospects of Danish language and humour in the future Europe.

I hope to satisfy both sides with this book, whilst emphasizing that the following represents my very own perception of this quite comprehensive matter.

As I see it, a description of the Danes would be incomplete and partly incomprehensible if I did not include our nearest sister nations, where necessary.

Great dramatic works require clearly defined characters, who stand or fall by what they believe in, and do not avoid conflicts. Therefore Norway and Sweden have such brillant playwrights as Ibsen, Bjørnson, Strindberg, Bergman, Norén. To be a poet however, one doesn't need to be particularly concerned about the world as such, as long as one keeps a constant eye on oneself and is able to maintain and express one's fascination for this image. This is why we have so few playwrights, but many poets in Denmark. And since these poets (I am one of them) are constantly engaged in this task, which could be defined as asking, »Who am I?« – without ever reaching any actual conclusion, as this would certainly mean the end of a writing career – we can never come to a decision as to what Danish mentality is all about.

However, from the above, the diligent reader will already have perceived one, maybe *the* infallible characteristic of every Dane:

We are champions at speaking derogatively of ourselves in a manner that serves to emphasize how magnificent we really are.

No one has expressed this more precisely than Hans Christian Andersen in his story, The Rags: Two rags, one Norwegian and one Danish, meet in a bundle of rags piled up outside a clothing factory.

»I am Norwegian!«, said the Norwegian rag, »and when I say that I'm Norwegian I think I've said enough!« ... »It tickles me in my fibres just to think of what I am ...«

The Danish rag replies: »A Danish rag could never speak in such a manner, It's against our nature. I know myself, and like me so are all our rags. We're so good-natured, so modest, we think too little of ourselves, and one doesn't really gain very much by this, but it pleases me so, I find it so charming! I can assure you, by the way, that I'm fully aware of my own worth, but I don't talk about it, no one can accuse me of such a flaw. I am soft and pliable, can tolerate anything, envy none, speak well of every one, although there isn't much good to say about the majority of others, but that's their problem. I just make fun of it all because I'm so intelligent!«

This self-ironic view of Danish mentality did not prevent Hans Christian Andersen and other Danish poets of the Golden Age from openly confessing their love of their country in delightful songs and poems. For a contemporary Danish poet, the situation is quite different; to avoid being made a laughingstock by fellow poets and countrymen one must maintain an ambivalent relationship to one's country; keep one's patriotism under cover and concentrate on scepticism and criticism.

And, if I am really to impress my fellow countrymen, I must resort to a sort of collective self-spanking, as will become clear. We Danes are so proud of our alleged humour and relaxed attitudes, that even our sister nations consider us a country of happy circus clowns:

SMILE

I was born with a howl
squalling I received my baptism
cried when I was beaten
screamed when bees stung me
but gradually became more Danish
learned to smile to the world
to the photographer
         to doctors
             policemen and perverts
became a citizen in the land of the smile
smiles keep the flies away and the mind clean
and light and air are good for the teeth
if you arrive too late
if you go bankrupt
if you are run over
just smile
tourists flock
to see smiling traffic victims
chuckling homeless
cackling bereaved

I cannot get my smile off
sometimes I feel like crying
or to just stand droopy-mouthed
or protest against other smiles
which conceal bloodthirst and rot
but my own smile gets in the way
sticks out like a car bumper
tearing hats and glasses off people
I bear my smile with a smile
         my crescent yoke
on which worries are hung out to dry
I must lean my head sideways

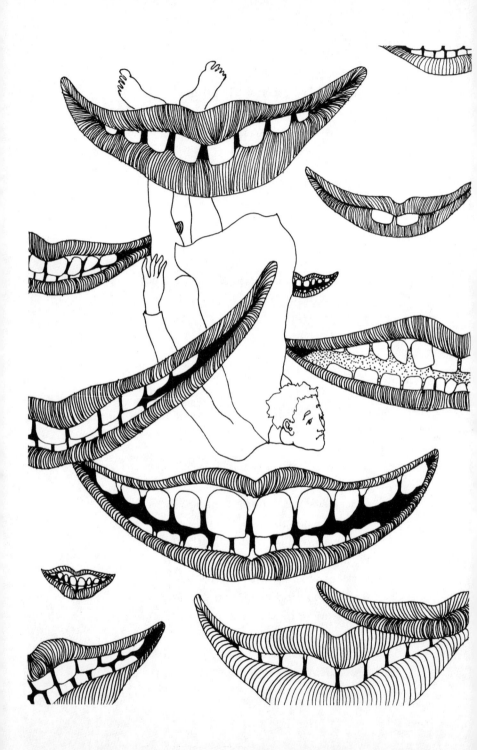

when I go through a door
I am a citizen in the land of the smile
It is not at all funny.

Another of our great poets of the Golden Age – and furthermore the source of inspiration for the Danish Folk High School – is N.F.S. Grundtvig. He is one of our finest hymn writers and also the author of many other songs loved by the Danes. In one of them, FAR HIGHER MOUNTAINS, he compares the splendour of the large countries with little, modest Denmark. But like a true patriot he concludes that Denmark, nevertheless, is the best of all countries where »few have too much and fewer too little«. That song inspired me to write this poem:

FAR FLATTER FIELDS

As a Dane one should sometimes
tear one's feet off the ground
          and take to the mountains
train in vision and vertigo.
Typical for mountains are peaks
but also the steep slopes
which make it possible to reach them.
It is healthy to learn
that life can be
so violent and unlikely
yes, almost hysterical.
You learn to think twice
when reading about foreign countries.
And you appreciate your own country more
when you return and see
how practical it actually is
that the fields are lying down.

A small country like Denmark naturally wishes to remain on friendly terms with its neighbour countries, big and small. This fact has played a part in the gradual development of a special Danish talent – peace negotiating. In fact, it could be considered more than a »talent«: The Danes feel called upon to act as good peace negotiators.

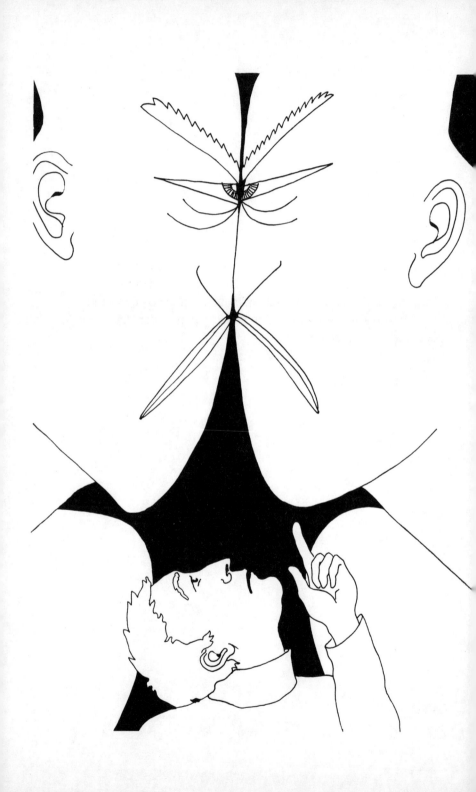

DEAR FRIENDS

I have two friends
who are enemies
and two enemies
who are friends.
One of my friends is a friend of one of my enemies.
My other friend is an enemy of my other enemy's friend.
It is difficult to keep track of
whom one should be careful not to say what to.
A reconciliation would simplify things considerably
so I strongly go in for
turning the other cheek
but in the long run haven't enough cheeks
try to mobilize my friends' cheeks.
This has made one of my enemies friendly
and one of my friends unfriendly.
My other enemy has become an enemy of his friend
and my other friend has become a friend of my
other enemy's former friend
but then an enemy of his own former friend.
I seriously consider calling the whole thing off
pulling my cheeks in
and starting afresh.

The following poem poses the question: Does the peace nego-
tiator arrive too late, or does the right moment occur immediately he arrives?

TO ONE WHO THREW A CHAIR

You stood with the chair lifted when I arrived.
I was out of breath.
You had rung me up.
Your eyes protruded
and your teeth when you shouted:
»Four years of my life I have wasted on her!
Is there anything as cold as a woman
who is otherwise warm!
For four years I have loved her!«
I never got a chance to say
anything.
You shouted:
»Out of my life!«
and threw the chair.
Not the window!
I managed to think.

Here is a list of
what I never managed to say:

1) Four years needn't be wasted
   consider them a gift
   you might otherwise have missed
2) I have two tickets to Count Basie
3) That is just the chair I have been looking for
4) Someday the two of us will laugh at this
5) Hold that pose while I fetch my camera
6) Can you lend me a hundred dollars
7) You are holding that chair wrong
8) When two mirrors mirror each other
   do they mirror their own mirror images

or do they mirror the reflection
of the other mirror's mirror image?
9) Your fly is open

But most important was
that I got there
just before the chair was thrown
and shattered against the wall
between two windows.
The most important thing is a faithful friend
who watches
when you throw your chair.

Who am I? How do I go on with my life? These are questions which naturally come to mind in crisis situations, when you feel your life has come to an abrupt standstill. But it is probably just as productive to ask, as the Dane in the following poem: Where am I and how did I get here?

The »big city« is Copenhagen, while the »suburb« is Søborg/Vangede, where I grew up.

THIS IS

This is the big city where we live
This is the small street in the big city where we live
This is the old house in the small street in the big city
where we live

This is you in that house
yes this is you
and this is me
in the middle of a sentence
in the middle of a TO that stretches in all directions
like a caterpillar at the end of a straw
This is the TO which twirls around at the end of something
which for the moment extends no further
like a mast-acrobat I saw as a child
the mast was high and lanky and swayed
eight metres to either side according to my father
I got a pain in my neck from looking so high
but escaped more cheaply than the daredevil
who later
or was it his predecessor
broke mast and neck
This is the neck that bears the head that remembers the neck
that sooner or later fell from the swaying mast
and snapped against the pavement of the street in the suburb
where I stretched my neck towards the presumptuous
and from this stems my later weakness for climbing
shipmasts telephone poles possibly streetlights
This is the pupated person
who came from that child by the mast in the suburb
to the big city where we live
that swaying Capital at the end of the street
that went through my clinging suburb
my neck-aching childhood
my trial-climbing youth

This is the spine that leads to the neck
that bears the head that uses the eyes
that saw the swaying acrobat at the end of the mast
in the suburb that clings to the big overpopulated city
$$\text{where we live}$$
This is the head that sways atop of the still erect spine
before you
eight thoughts to either side
These are your eyes that are focused on the TO
that I saw at the end of the swaying mast
in the childhood I have now climbed up from
to the point where I can go no further
This is the TO
and this is you
yes, this is you
Lend me a little finger.

In the American Declaration of Independence it says, ... **that all men are created equal**. I completely agree with this. But how is this noble idea implemented?

In Denmark we have already solved the problem in our own special way.

EQUALITY

And no human beings are inferior
That some feel inferior
and feel others as superior
is mainly due to the fact
that those who feel superior
cause others to feel inferior
Making others feel inferior
must be considered as inferior
so therefore those who consider themselves
superior and others as inferior
must themselves be considered inferior
But if everyone is to be considered as inferior
the characterization becomes useless
thus there are no longer any inferior human beings
                   here on the reservation.

In countries with democratic traditions – like Denmark – the citizens may have a tendency to take democracy for granted, a natural right, which it should well be, but definitely is not. Even a quick glance at the development in Europe and other parts of the world shows, with all undesirable clarity, how vulnerable and fragile democracy still is. It must be constantly mastered, maintained, further developed and defended, not only on an official level but also in the daily life of each citizen. For this purpose the following set of useful exercises are suggested.

16 BASIC EXERCISES IN DEMOCRATIC THINKING AND BEHAVIOUR

1. Brush your teeth at least three times a day. Observe which teeth you brush the most and which of them are your own.
2a. Take a bath. Turn off the tap when the water is approximately 20 cms from the rim of the tub. Estimate roughly the total number of drops in the tub. Pull out the plug and dry yourself thoroughly.
2b. Count the number of people on earth. Subtract them.
3a. Imagine that, for a whole week, you would only be able to express yourself by means of pumpernickel.
3b. Then, prepare sandwiches for your children's school lunch.
4. At short intervals put your finger in the ground. See if it takes root.
5. Observe what makes people sing and what makes them stop. Write a song that begins where they stop.
6a. Imagine that you are neither standing beside democracy's grave, nor beside its cradle, but in the midst of its blossoming puberty.
6b. Imagine there is a long way yet to go.
6c. Imagine that the long way is the shortest.
6d. Imagine that the longest way is to remain where you are.
7. Describe roughly springtime introduced as a Bill of Law.
8. Write 12 times – distinctly, preferably in capital letters: »I will fight to the end of my days for my opponent's right to take the floor and express his nonsense.«
9. Put different flowers in a vase, arrange them according to colour, fragrance, height, etc., so each flower is seen at its best. Having done this write a letter to the bouquet and explain the principles of your arrangement.
10. Particularly during thunder storms: Be aware that the

lightning conductor stems from the lightning, not the other way round.

11a. Read about the Pyramids and about the slaves who dragged the stones up them.

11b. Read about Sisyphus who pushed a stone up the mountain in vain.

11c. Walk around your house – or your bicycle – and see if there is anything that needs to be repaired.

12a. Draw a semicircle. To the left of the paper where the semicircle begins, write: SILENCE. To the right, where the arc ends write: TO TALK ONE'S HEAD OFF or BLABBER. On top of the arc, in the centre, write: TO SAY SOMETHING. Then try to place the Members of Parliament (without consideration to political colour) on this arc.

12b. Try to place yourself on this arc.

12c. Put away the paper and repeat the exercise three months later, one year later, and four years later.

13. Imagine that Denmark is governed by 1) pharmacists 2) right-foot boxers 3) Vikings.

14. Imagine that you are 1) your wife/husband 2) one of your children 3) a Greenlander 4) yourself.

15 Try to play the first movement of the Moonlight Sonata with one finger (minus pedal).

16. Watch a sunrise occasionally, while you breathe in long deep rhythmical breaths from the very bottom of your lungs and hold your shoulders completely relaxed. As you inhale, say to yourself: »I give a damn about nothing!« – and as you exhale: »There is something good about SOMETHING!«

Like most people the Dane longs for his home when abroad. However, his return home can be very problematic as Denmark is a country in rapid development. 40% of the population still lived in rural areas in 1900. In 1940 the number had dropped to 25%. Today it is under 5%. That is why people who emigrated around 40 to 50 years ago have difficulty identifying today's hectic, noisy Denmark with their idyllic dreams of a country inhabited by farmers, artisans and fishermen.

But even for a contemporary, resident Dane, it can be frustrating to realize that his country couldn't even stay put the short time he was abroad.

HOME AGAIN

You feel it the moment you have landed
the air a little warmer than when you went abroad
scent of clover and hawthorn and grass pollen
the acoustics spiced with returned voices
starlings swallows and peewits
nothing is quite the same as before

On your way through the city new
signs between old familiar ones
a bookshop transformed into McDonald's
a flowershop into a videoshop
a market place into a parking lot
nothing is quite the same as before

Most acquaintances look the same however
apart from minor deviations
one has lost weight another has gained some
a few are dead others are newborn
one has got a car another grey hair
nothing is quite the same as before

But life goes on and
that's just fine
or whatever it is
it would've been rather absurd if everything
had come to a standstill because you were away
and everything was quite the same as before

No, life goes on and
that's just fine
or whatever it is
so why this sharp stab of pain
or whatever it is because
nothing is quite the same as before

Had you expected that everything stood still like
Sleeping Beauty's palace because you went away
that everything remained the same
and the future was postponed
until you returned
and everything was again the same as before

Observe your loved ones' loving smiles
your friends' happiness at seeing your face again
feel yourself missed and loved and watch them drink in
each word from your mouth while they
burst with sheer desire to tell their stories
because nothing is quite the same as before

You hadn't really expected them to renounce
all earthly pleasure while you were away
you don't really mean they should've abstained
from food sleep and sex and welcomed you
like bare skeletons because then nothing
would really be the same as before

No but at the same time they don't seem
to have wanted for anything
and when a few months change so much
how about the day when you're really dead
and probably feel like haunting a bit
and nothing is quite the same as before

Live while alive and envy not
but wish the living all possible life
a hand can be clenched as well as opened
use it to caress and not to strike
tomorrow could probably be another day
where nothing is quite the same as before.

This rapid development in society, this forced tempo is reflected in the smallest social unit – the nuclear family.

One day my daughter got married. For some reason or other this event always takes the bride's father by surprise, and I was no exception. In my memory it seemed only a few weeks since she was a little schoolgirl with a pony-tail and a skipping-rope. Suddenly a strange young man had carried her off and married her!

I was never the same again. Actually, neither was she.

TIME

We have twelve clocks in our house
still there's never enough time
You go into the kitchen
get chocolate milk for your spindly son
but when you return
he has grown too old for chocolate milk
demands beer girls revolution
You must make the most of your time while you have it
Your daughter comes home from school
goes out to play hopscotch
comes in a little later
and asks if you will mind the baby
while she and her husband go to the theatre
and while they are at the theatre
the child with some difficulty
is promoted to 10th grade
You must make the most of your time while you have it
You photograph your hitherto young wife
with full-blooded gipsy headscarf
an opulent fountain in the background
but the picture is hardly developed
before she announces that it is soon
her turn to collect old age pension
softly the widow awakes in her
You would like to make the most of your time
but it gets lost all the time
where has it gone
was it ever there at all
have you spent too much time
drawing time out
You must make the most of time in time
roam around for a time without time and place
and when it's time

call home and hear
»You have called 95 94 93 92?
That number is no longer available.«
Click.

Allow me, just for a moment, to suppress my indoctrinated, Danish false modesty; the reason is that I am often called one of the most Danish poets in Denmark. For years I have fought against this label in vain. One of my most popular books is titled SVANTE'S SONGS. It has been spoken of as the perfect picture of Danish mentality, despite the fact that the main character is originally a Swede. He grew up in Denmark, but was quite frustrated over being involuntarily Danish.

Hence this poem which questions who the real Danes are.

CLOSET SWEDES

Is there anything as Danish as a potato?
The potato stems from South America.

Is there anything as Danish as the Dannebrog itself?
It fell from heaven in Estonia a long time ago
and resembles the Swiss flag.

Does anything sound more genuinely Danish
than the music of the ballad-opera »Elverhøj«?
Composed by a German with frequent use
of Swedish folk tunes.

Be careful
now it becomes difficult:
Is there anyone more Danish than the Danes?
Descendants of the Danes
a tribe in Sweden
who invaded our country sometime in the third century A.D.
while the original Danes
the Herules
the noble and brave
but outnumbered Herules
were driven to flight by the terrible Swedish Danes
had to roam displaced around ancient Europe
for several centuries until finally
a few thousand of these original Danes succeeded
in reaching Sweden where they settled
under the dubious name *Swedes*

Here is the question once again
and think carefully before you answer:
Is there anyone more Danish than the Danes?

The correct answer is:
Yes!
The Swedes!
They are the authentic primeval Danes
Like the Jews in the wilderness
they are constantly drawn to the promised land
which flows with beer and bacon
but has been occupied for seventeen hundred years
By whom?
By the Swedes!
By us!

No wonder that Scania
demands to have Denmark back
no wonder that many of us Crypto-Swedes
have difficulty speaking proper Danish
cut off suffixes
swallow consonants
choke on syntax
so everything sounds like »Rødgrød med fløde«
no wonder that we hardly understand each other
no wonder that the most frequently used word is »what?«
It is not at all our language
We are not at all us
We are a bunch of bloody Swedish foreign workers
who have wrecked this lovely country
why don't we go back to where we come from
home to Sweden
»Thy sun, thy skies, thy verdant meadows smiling«
where at last we could acknowledge our true identity
show our colours
»We are yellow
We are blue«
Where we could decisively beat ourselves at football
and defeat ourselves in the European Song Contest

Oh, how we have needed
and longed for this
at last to be able to sing Bellman's ballads
in their original language
or *språk* as it is actually called
at last to have the exclusive right
of being the only ones in the world
who can faultlessly pronounce
Sjutusensjuhundrasjutisju
without losing our dentures
finally to be freed from our
frustrating national inferiority complex
and be allowed to spread our wings
and soar to the skies
as the freest Nordic swans
At last we can be rid of continuous blame
for that stupid Jante's Law
which some crazy Norwegian writer
has saddled upon us

At last ourselves
at last free
»Thou ancient, thou freeborn«
at last home where we belong
at last to have a chance
to make a Half a Whole
and generously drink a toast to ourselves
as soon as we have introduced humane conditions
concerning alchohol
The drinking songs are already available
now is the time to fulfil them
make them trustworthy

Great times ahead
and
If we can make it here
we'll make it everywhere

And after all
there is far more space in Sweden.

What I find most lacking among my countrymen is an element of craziness, of excessiveness. We are so decent, so matter-of-fact, so predictable.

Our Nordic brothers meet the ups and downs of life each with his own variety of ethnic madness: the exuberant megalomania of the Norwegian, the sudden flash of schizophrenia in the Swedes, the Finns' introvert autism illuminated by perpetual northern lights.

While the Dane says, »Well, everything will probably soon be alright – why don't we just talk things over …«

But one day I was asked by a chef, the owner of one of our finest restaurants, for permission to print my poem *Diet* on his menu card.

That gave me new hope for the future of the nation.

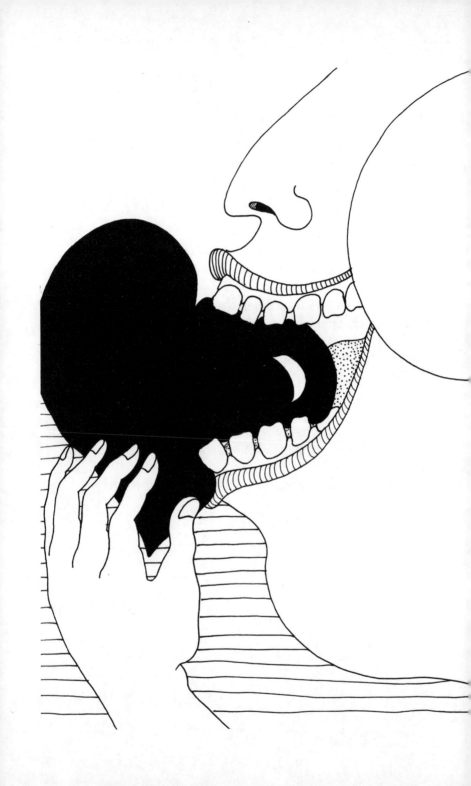

DIET

Shrimps will shrink your corneas
lard will give you pimples
pancakes lie too flat in the stomach
pork isn't good for the heart
fish isn't good for the butcher
chicken isn't good for the chicken
meatballs aren't good for anything
Avoid sago soup during pregnancy
avoid onions during marriage
sweet is sinful
sour is dangerous
salt shortens life
bitter drags it out
marmalade gives flabby ears
stew contracts the swim-bladder
eggs make the arms sit awry
cheese affects your sense of smell
horseradish affects your taste
biscuits affect your hearing
radishes narrow your horizon
peas stop development
cauliflower blocks the view
breakfast spoils the appetite
late meals sharpen it
food isn't good for the stomach
life is unhealthy
munch
munch
munch

As previously mentioned, it can become tiresome always to be considered a typical Danish poet: »You are so very Danish – it must be impossible to translate your work.« – I who want so much to come out into the world. It feels stifling.

But, on a few rare occasions, I must admit it is not entirely wrong. Once on a visit to sunny southern Italy, happily far from restless, rainy Copenhagen, I felt like capturing the atmosphere in a poem. And presto! Note where my chalky inner self steers his rattling steps: towards the Royal Theatre in Copenhagen.

THE REBELLIOUS SKELETON

In a way I quite understand my skeleton
When I lie sunbathing it is never allowed
to come out in the sun for a little while
it must feel humiliating
patronizing
all that manages
to stick out
are the few teeth I have left
and my short nails
otherwise it is only felt faintly like bumps
knuckles and knobs under the skin
plus a few kneecaps
the rest is reduced to a life in the shade
and as I lie there slowly dehydrating
I sense my skeleton's phosphorescent anger:
Yes, by all means keep lying down!
skeleton oppressor
old rib fascist
vertebra imperialist
keep lying down or better still
rot as fast as possible
so that I can free myself from you
and fulfil every skeleton's rightful dream
of dancing lightly across the meadows
with scythe in hand and smiling teeth
and empty eye sockets
ah! at last to be able to
rattle with all of one's proud bones
released from your flabby fat
mawkish bowels
sloppy brain
ah! at last to be able
unhindered to scare along the way

To get forward either here or there
just scare
ah! at last to be able to
rejoice at the screams of small children
rattle at the moon
clank at the sun
perhaps my jingling victory tour
will culminate on Kongens Nytorv
at the Royal Theatre
in a ballet by Flemming Flindt
or how about posing for a while
for a young and successful morbid painter
considering what I've had to put up with from you
so by all means keep lying down
you old bone racist
now my time has come
release all skeletons
Spring is here

Then I jump with a start
rush home
brush like mad
what teeth I have left to brush

I sympathise with my lifetime prisoner
wish I could do something
but am too much of a coward and too thin-skinned to
actually arrange a compound fracture of a shin bone
to give it a little glimpse of the world outside
but it will be long before
I cut my nails.

For hundreds and hundreds of years the Danish language, like several other European languages, has been very open. It has adopted and welcomed words from many other languages. Thousands and thousands of foreign words have immigrated into our language, have developed and enriched it, have become naturalized.

The following poem can be perceived as an appeal to my own country, as well as other European countries: Let us be just as open-minded as our languages are!

COSMOPOLITAN IN DENMARK

As a child
I learned good old Danish children's dances
with exotic names
Scottische
Rhinelander Polka
Tyrolienne
The Lancers
As a young man: modern waltz
Argentinian tango
Brazilian samba
but I dance them quite Danish

I was confirmed in a religion
which comes from the Middle East
Grew up with Hans Christian Andersen's fairy tales
as well as with Grimm's
and Arabian Nights
Aladdin and the Wonderful Lamp
The Magic Carpet
Sinbad the Sailor
Ali Baba and the Forty Thieves
Open, Sesame!

When I wrote my first love letters
I never carved runes
like my Nordic ancestors
actually I'm rather bad at runes
I used the Roman alphabet
and this she understood very well!

I drink Java coffee and Ceylon tea
French claret
Spanish sherry

Scottish Scotch
West Indian rum
Russian vodka
but no matter how much I drink
I sing »Sejle op ad åen« in Danish!

And the language I sing and speak
is woven together with words from the whole world
not only from German, English and French
No, listen to my Greenlandic:
Anorak – kayak – tupilac
Turkish: yoghurt – kiosk
Finnish: sauna
Arabian: almanac – coffee
Chinese: tea
Mexican: tomato
Australian: boomerang – kangaroo
South African: apartheid
I could go on and on – and so I shall:
Japanese: kimono – karate
Malayan: bamboo
Hindi: bungalow – pyjamas
I can repeat them in my sleep
Words from all over this revolving globe
meet in my marvellous mouth
and each time I pronounce them
they sound more and more Danish

My shirt is from India
my shoes from Italy
my car from Japan
my watch is from Switzerland – or Hong Kong
but in the midst of it all I am so thoroughly Danish
The whole world gathers in me
and is perfectly blended!

Sesame, Sesame
Open, Sesame …
Or is it I who am Sesame?
At any rate I will open up!

It is easier for the arts of music and painting to cross borders than literature, for example – national as well as social and cultural borders.

To a certain degree, the same applies to love. But where music and painting can be shared by many, the experience of true love is something unique. At least this is how it is experienced during the most blissful moments: No other person on planet earth has ever loved another person the way I love you.

THE FACE ABOUT THE FACE

There are many things I can imagine different
a different summer in Denmark
different prices on books and beer
a different government
perhaps redhaired
a different Copenhagen
(but too late
Copenhagen IS already different)
A different typewriter
a different poem
a different world
which no one wanted different
Peace on earth I can imagine
as well as the end of the world
Everything I can imagine different
or if not exactly everything
at least I can imagine
that I can imagine everything different
Everything
but your face
Your face I cannot imagine different
well, maybe a little more plump or thin
but not your eyes in another face
not your face with other eyes
not your voice from other lips
How have I become so conservative
I who go in for a change of the world
I can imagine your face
a little older
much older
115 years
shrunken head
grey mane rumpled

by my bony hand
That I have imagination for
I can surely imagine
your face different
your face as such
but not THAT about your face
which makes it just your face
the special thing about your face
the face about your face
I cannot imagine your face different
That's the terrible thing about it
It's just as well!

The paradox of love (and true love is always a paradox) is, however, that this devotion for the one and only, this belief in the exclusive, in itself contains the key to the communal. The possibility for a richer life: Just as a small country can survive by opening up towards the world at large, the individual citizen can break his emotional isolation by welcoming life's most important immigration: Love.

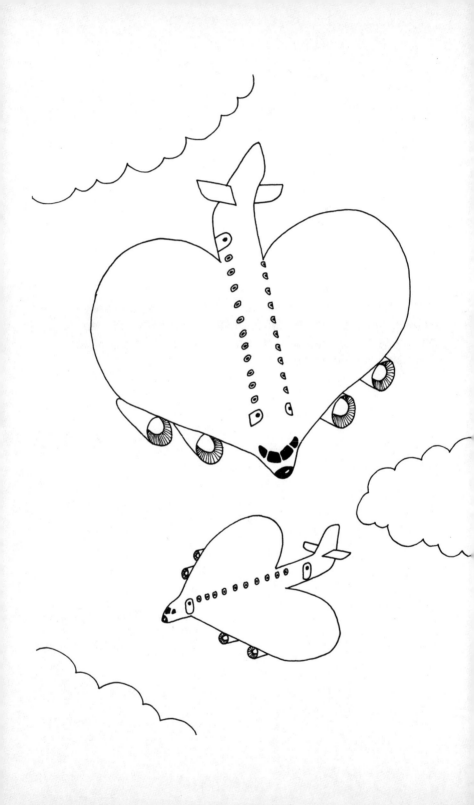

IMMIGRANT INTO MY HEART

I met you as a stranger
but discovered that you knew me
better than I did

You took me on a voyage into myself
you knew short cuts
to overlooked views
and underlooked coral reefs
What on my map said
DEAD END
turned out to be ways to the mind's largest
and most loving airport

You took measurements of my daily horizon
and while I sat as on pins and needles
you saw your chance
to pull the pins and needles out
and use them in your pattern
you cut and pieced out
and expanded my old ready-made horizon
by several thousand kilometres
so it wasn't too tight around life

Not until late into the night
you nodded satisfied:
»At first it will feel
a trifle loose around the past
but it is designed to grow in
and it suits you really well!«

My life's redoubler
immigrant into my heart
with little too wide

slightly floppy horizons
I embrace you
on this intimate night of Spring.

But, also seen in a more universal perspective, we are all immigrants. And emigrants.

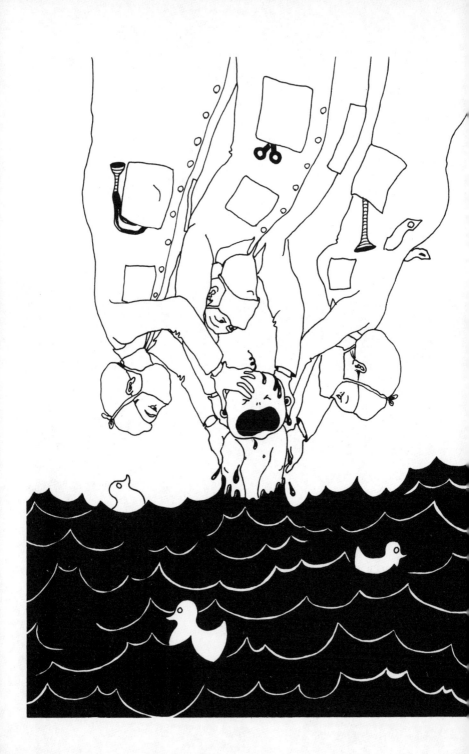

MY LIFE AS AN IMMIGRANT

It was a dark and cold November morning
when I came into the world
a little freezing immigrant into the North
expelled from my tropical abode
with an average temperature of
almost 38 degrees centigrade in the shade
where I could bathe safely day and night
in my little warm two pints' ocean

My earliest life
embraced by warmth
gently lapping well-being
a woman's voice humming
later turned out to be my mother's
and a playful strumming on strings
which made me somersault in the water
I recognized later as my father's banjo
everything was here
and need not be understood

Imagine the shock
when suddenly I was expelled
from my tropical Paradise
and deported to an Arctic region
perhaps it was 20 degrees
perhaps 21
on the maternity ward of Denmark's National Hospital
but to me it was beastly cold
stark naked as I was
an icy cold and bone dry nightmare
and then the shouting voices
in an unintelligible language
white-clad giants turned me upside down

slapped me on my poor bottom
which only knew warm caressing ripples
and since babies already have difficulty
telling the difference between up and down
I became even more confused by
this crowd of noisy lunatics
who stood on their heads
waving arms in the air
with bared teeth

Help
I thought
Now I'm done for
I thought
I've landed among savages
I thought
is it so strange that I screamed
and the more I screamed
the louder they shouted
they fought over me
scraped the last warm moisture off me
with extremely dry cloths
pure torture
I screamed and screamed
Am – am – mam
I couldn't pronounce
Amnesty International
but that wouldn't have helped either
Amnesty International didn't exist then
that cold and dark November morning
in the crisis and collapse year 1929
when I was expelled into this cold world

But gradually I became assimilated
learnt the quite funny language

grew up
settled down
got work a car and family
gradually became one of them
even dreamed in their language
became attached to this strange country
although not everything that goes on here
has my entire approval
however on longer journeys abroad
I often catch myself sending
wistful thoughts towards the country
as if it were from whence I came
from where my world had sprung
while the memory of my first home
my maternal lagoon
became a distant unreal dream
a gently lapping humming legend
a soft murmur in the deep conch of the mind

Now I have reached the age
where I can count the years till
I shall once again be expelled
to another world
learn another new language
study new customs which
compared to everything I know
probably is a non-language
and certain non-customs
until now we have only received very vague
and inconsistent information
apparently anything can be expected
not to mention nothing
I wonder if it's quite as cold and noisy
as on arrival in my present country
will I also be welcomed there at the border

by a crowd of white-clad noisy lunatics
turned upside down
or is it as hot as hell and silent
nobody to welcome you
are you yourself a nobody
whom other nobodies aren't there to welcome
The only reliable reports we have about the place
is that contrary to
several other countries
it has a highly developed and tolerant
immigrant and refugee policy
extremely seldom
is anyone rejected at the border.

What we in Denmark call *Wienerbrød* (Vienna bread) is called *Danish Pastry* in English. This applies to cakes and biscuits as well as a number of other things. On closer inspection, many national specialities often turn out to be inspired from abroad.

In return, the following description of a very early phase in the baking process itself may evoke sweet memories across the borders.

CAKE BATTER

When the grown-ups baked cakes on Sundays
sister-cakes angel-cakes crullers
when they had mixed the batter in a bowl
and scooped it up into a baking tin
and they let you have the bowl
you stood with happiness itself in your hands
scraped with a finger the abundant remains
of the most delicious batter
and licked it off your finger
a golden sweetness
marzipan and honey and motherly warmth
which at that very moment
with all of a child's wonderful clairvoyance
you realized would never be surpassed
by any other earthly dish
and indeed you were right

The peculiar thing about it was
and is
that the grown-ups were unaware of this
that they preferred to blend this heavenly batter
transformed it into ordinary cakes
which tasted good
admittedly
but were only
primitive stiffened reproductions
of this thick-flowing love
which warmed the cockles of your mouth
and from within lit up your tummy
like the banquet hall of a fairy castle
It was really a mystery to me
why the grown-ups
immediately after the batter was made

didn't send us children out to play
and threw themselves over the batter
and fought for it
of course I kept my mouth shut about this
I had better use for my mouth
but to this day it remains a mystery to me.

When compared with children in many other countries, Danish children are brought up more freely. The sceptics claim that this pedagogic theory tends to confuse children and make them restless, whereas learning by heart, fixed limits and discipline is better for them.

Quite the opposite, say the supporters: Robot-like discipline and passive learning by heart stunts the natural development of children. It is better to encourage children's innate creativity and ability to think independently, so they can become aware, active citizens in a modern democracy. Not »yes, sir«, but rather »why, Peter?« (Or Maria, Lisa or Hans, because Danish children call their teachers by their first names, which also shocks many foreign visitors.)

DIDACTIC POEM
(for teachers and other adults)

To teach can soon become to prune.
Let the children's curiosity grow.
It's not enough that they know what YOU know.
Moreover, you should take inspiration
from their thirst for experimentation
with colours, tones, things and words.
The lesson is short.
The world is vast.
Rejection creates
a future loser.
Loving care has much more to say
to a growing mind
than the lesson today.
That is what's hard to understand:
YOU can learn from the future man.
Call to mind the creative zest
you as a child yourself possessed.

However, it seems to me that modern methods of upbringing tend to neglect an important dimension, and the following can be perceived as my modest, but rather essential, contribution to future child-upbringing:

Occasionally, small children find it natural to sit and think of nothing and everything, withdraw into themselves and become one with nature and the cosmos. What in a posh word is called *meditation*.

This behaviour is frowned upon in our modern result-pursuing society. Immediately along comes an over-zealous parent or teacher: »Don't just sit there! Do something sensible! Do your homework! Or go out and play with the other children!«

As a result, this talent withers away during children's growth. Later in adult life, when a need for pause and meditation arises, they must take expensive courses to re-learn the art in which they excelled as small children, quite free of charge.

Therefore this request to Danish children. And all other children around the world.

DAY-DREAM

Day-dream
my child
just day-dream
sit and stare out into the air
at a wall
at a fly
at nothing
be absent
be away
for a moment
or hours
for everything there is a time
a time to work
a time to grow
a time for outward
a time for inward
a time to embrace
a time to day-dream
so day-dream
my child

The grown-ups around you
would rather run into a brick wall
than sit and day-dream
restlessly they make plans
gloat when they succeed
despair when they fail
act and react
scuttle to and fro
are always exactly where they started
constantly take up burning topics of the day
and quickly drop them
as if they were burning

onwards onwards!
away away!
to repeat oneself
is beginning senility
for concentration
life is too short
to day-dream
is anti-social
onwards onwards!
away away!

When the grown-ups meet themselves in a dream
they do not recognize the image
startled they scream
nightmare!
a sleeping pill
what could it have been
those shrimps must have been off

So day-dream now
my child
while there is time
before you become like one of us
who restlessly gather distractions
and have forgotten to day-dream.

Other Danes will have each his or her own special view of the Danes. But, as is evident from this book, I have not only wanted to give my personal description of my countrymen; though I am extremely nearsighted, I have also tried to use my spectacles much like binoculars into the next millenium, and have focused my eyes on what I think is the future for us Danes.

SECLUDED PLACES ARE NOT
WHAT THEY USED TO BE

You search for a word
and find a language

You kiss a mouth
and marry a people

You dig in the garden
and bump into a planet

You look up surprised
and you are Springtime.

NOTES TO CLOSET SWEDES

Rødgrød med fløde: a term which means something like *Red Jell-o with cream*, but that is less important here. This phrase is a test put to all foreigners by the Danes. If you can pronounce these words correctly, you have proved that you're a real Dane. If not, you're on very thin ice.

Sjutusensjuhundrasjuttisju: Swedish for *seventhousandseven-hundredandseventyseven.* This is a similar Swedish linguistic test. If you pronounce it correctly you may be a sort of Swede. If not, you are most certainly a Dane.

Jante's Law: The originator of Jante's law was the Danish-Norwegian writer Aksel Sandemose. This law has been called The Ten Commandments of Mediocrity – or of self-suppression. Actually, the entire Danish nation felt touched to the quick and still feels very wronged by this law. Among its most important commandments are these two:
You shall not think that you are anything
You shall not think that you are better than us

Scania: Skåne, the south-western part of Sweden. Belonged to Denmark until the middle of the 17th century.

Thy sun, thy sky, thy verdant meadows smiling: a quotation from the Swedish national anthem.

Thou ancient, thou freeborn: Title of the Swedish national anthem *DU GAMLA, DU FRIA.*

Make a Half a Whole: refers to a well-known Swedish drinking song, *Helan går* (the first schnapps goes) actually a fascinating, but very exhausting schnapps ritual, depending on how many glasses each person is courageous enough to consume.

NOTE TO COSMOPOLITAN IN DENMARK

Sejle op ad åen: Old popular refrain, known by all Danes and sung on festive occasions in a form of neverending mass mantra:

> *Sailing up the river*
> *sailing down again*
> *what a lovely song this is*
> *let us sing it once again: We are*
> *Sailing up the river* ... (repeated for hours and hours)

GENERAL NOTES

These poems have been printed previously in the original Danish in:

Smile – *Den indre bowlerhat*, 1964
Far Flatter Fields – *Personlige papirer*, 1974
Dear Friends – *Det sidste øh*, 1969
To One Who Threw a Chair – *Under begge øjne*, 1978
This Is – *Portrætgalleri*, 1966
Equality – *Her i reservatet*, 1971
16 Basic Exercises in Democratic Thinking and Behaviour –
                             Demokrati (Gyldendal) 1980
Home Again – *Denne kommen og gåen*, 1993
Time – *Her i reservatet*, 1971
Closet Swedes – *Chagall & skorpiondans*, 1991
Diet – *Den indre bowlerhat*, 1964
The Rebellious Skeleton – *Denne kommen og gåen*, 1993
Cosmopolitan in Denmark – *Over adskillige grænser*, 1988
The Face about the Face – *Himmelspræt eller Kunsten at*
                             komme til verden, 1979
Immigrant into My Heart – *Denne kommen og gåen*, 1993
My Life as an Immigrant – *Denne kommen og gåen*, 1993
Cake Batter – *Denne kommen og gåen*, 1993
Didactic Poem – *Barndommens land*, Brugsens kalender, 1990
Day-Dream – *Tiden og Storken*, 1985
Secluded Places Are Not What They Used to Be –
                             Denne kommen og gåen, 1993